John Mason

Signposts

Poems from here, there & elsewhere

Cannon Poets Publishing

First published 2016 by Cannon Poets Publishing

Cannon Poets Publishing
22 Margaret Grove
Harborne
Birmingham B17 9JH

http://www.cannonpoets.org.uk

A CIP catalogue entry for this book is available from the British Library.

ISBN 978-0-9538900-1-9

Cover Design: Laura Mason

All proceeds from the sale of this book will be donated to the
Alzheimer's Society

In aid of

Alzheimer's Society

Leading the
fight against
dementia

CONTENTS

PART 2 CIRCLING CONTINENTS

PART 3 MISCELLANY

ACKNOWLEDGEMENTS and INTRODUCTION

My thanks go to Connie Ramsey Bott and Cathy Whittaker for rekindling a spark for poetry; to Don Barnard for throwing fuel on the fire and introducing me to Cannon Poets; to Connie's Open Mind sessions for her continuing challenges; to all friends and colleagues at Cannon Poets, Warwick Words Writers Group and Coventry Live Poets, for their company and stimulation.

Special thanks to Connie, Martin Underwood and Eleanor Nesbitt for their constructive comments. Particular thanks are due to *Cannon Poets Publishing* and particularly to Greg Cox and Martin Underwood for their encouragement and support. Some of the poems in this book have previously appeared in *The Cannon's Mouth*.

I express my gratitude to Bob Peake for his expert knowledge and his family for hospitality in the course of two walks following the River Wye; for help and hospitality on the Oxford Canal thanks go to Sylvia and Barrie Shield, late of Rugby and to Joy and Norman Drake of Deddington; and to Alaric Pritchard for his assistance in Newcastle.

I thank my grand-daughter Laura Mason for her front cover illustration, and Ros my wife and support for over 50 years, for her tolerance and patience.

ALZHEIMERS WALKS 2011- 2015

In 2011 having reached 70 years of age in reasonable mental and physical health, and having worked with staff from Alzheimer's Society locally in Coventry and Warwickshire I decided to go on a long distance walk (a new venture) and raise funds for Alzheimer's. This first walk covered the length of Offa's Dyke Path from Chepstow to Prestatyn and I was accompanied by my son David for the first few days. The success of this led to further walks: in 2012, the length of the River Wye Path, Chepstow to the top of Plynlimon; in 2013 the Oxford Canal from its start in north Coventry to Isis lock on the Thames in Oxford; in 2014 the Kennet and Avon Canal and the River Avon from its junction with the Thames in Reading to the last lock at Hanham where it becomes a tidal river; and in 2015 Hadrian's Wall from Newcastle upon Tyne to Bowness on Solway. I raised more than £6,000 in sponsorship donations from these walks which totalled over 600 miles.

In producing this book I have used some of the poems I wrote while on these walks and also on visits abroad which I have been fortunate enough to make.

Some of these poems reflect my own 'good times', many others reflect nothing more than my fevered imagination!

***

The first poem 'Talk to me of the Good Times' was written in response to a 2010 consultation meeting in Coventry about the design/redesign of facilities in the Dementia Ward at University Hospitals Coventry and Warwickshire, Coventry. I donated this to the local Alzheimer's staff and it has since been displayed in the Forget-Me-Not lounge of the Hospital's Dementia Ward.

Talk to Me of the Good Times

Tell me about the fun times
when I have gone to ground -

Talk to me of the sunshine
when I am confined in the dark -

Remind me of foolish laughter
when I am sad and far away -

Take me through the good days
when my eyes are dimmed -

Walk me back through woodlands
where I listened to birds -

Show me the rivers and fields
where once I roamed and played -

Replay me the sound of the ocean
now I am locked to the land -

Help me remember friends I've known
now that their faces fade -

Touch my hand and talk to me
though I forget your name -

I am still a human being
inside I am still the same.

1

ALZHEIMER'S WALKS

A Summer Lane

(on the Powys-Hereford border)

Fern-lined, a high-hedged lane pierced
by purpled foxglove, fireweed spires
of red rise in heated air; aromas
thicken: white puffs of meadowsweet,
woodbine (Louis Armstrong's favourite)
in full flower yellow pink,
and flooding from a field the smell
of new mown hay, sweet vernal grass -
I know I should go on but cannot pass;
stay, recline and rest, surrender
to the soporific perfume's power
and in this land of ancient Saints,
weak sinner that I am, delay marching on
to become one of that sainted number
for an hour; and after, walking every day
wear a honeysuckle sprig, a nosegay
to revive the flagging step,
bliss consumed with every breath.

On the Edge

High on the moors of Hatterall Ridge, wind-balanced
between England and Wales I tread heather, bilberried
paths over black peat masses. Pools hide, shining
through tufted greenery, shard-strewn with white
stones or bone, trodden by ponies, sheep and man,
ancients: wayfarer, shepherd, Norman and Welsh
vying for mastery, monks straying from valley-hugged
abbeys; and before - countless tribes who staked out
the high ground. I find shadowy faces deep in peat
waters, brown shimmers under white-mirrored skies
stare back as I puzzle, search for connections.
A hand beckons, reaches for mine until wind-borne
entreaties submerge under the weight of passing clouds.
I retreat uncertain, settle for now on firmer ground.

Signs of Life

Exposed in the high wildness
a signpost
rises from bracken –
all around turf
grazed by horses and sheep

The post tilts
its finger boards pointing
who knows where –
no indication of distance or place–
weather-worn wood, aged, eroded
but sustaining life

Surfaces covered by frayed discs
of bronze, silver, gold –
not medals nailed up to celebrate mere winners
runners-up in races but the survival of species –

patches of lichen, air-fed, tenacious,
finding a home, taking hold,
     settling in, facing
     sun and rain, wind,
         hail and snow –
    slow-growing
      slow
        slow
          so slow
that if you passed this way
next month
     next year
you would hardly know

The River Unk

(a real river in Shropshire)

When I arrived at the River Unk
To cross the bridge it had sunk,
(Not the bridge, the Unk).
All its water had shrunk
To nothing, done a bunk,
Not a drop to be seen or drunk;
Needn't have bought my swimming trunk
s, not even enough to dunk
A hot toe into. Bone dry, just pebbles – chunk
After chunk with an occasional hunk
Of bigger stone, but devoid of debris, junk.
You could have fallen in without making a clunk.
Some people may have thought it stunk
To come so far and find a riverless Unk
Such a minor test to flunk
But I didn't lose my head or funk.
It could have been worse was all I thunk
So I crossed the bridge and away I slunk.
This is all true, I'm no gossip, no quidnunc!

Moel Arthur

I sit at Moel Arthur's summit, sun-drenched,
a perfect spot, smaller yet shapelier
than nearby Mother Mountain, Moel Famau;
happy with my lot but tired among harsh
heather. I taste bilberry, breathe wild thyme,
while Snowden far away floats mistily.
Dream as Iron Age women, children busy on the hill
pick herbs, fruit, dig roots, gather kindling, cook,
scrape skins outside their homes while
in the woods below, logs, lodge-poles are hewn,
hauled uphill by short brawny men, dragged inside
their ditched defences where I sit alone in silence,
save for the hum of a single bumble-bee
and high above a circling buzzard's yelp.

I Thought of You Fondly

As I walked the length of my wild Welsh river
in rain and sun, heading back in time to its source
I thought fondly of you: our recent re-union
and times long past – you, lover of heights, wide spaces
now Devon-rooted, nestled deep in your valley
by your own running waters, your own mill-stream.

How we greeted crossing the field – Heathcliff and Cathy
in very slow motion, recognition instant in spite
of shape-shifting years – and embraced. Smile enigmatic,
eyes still bright, turning full-skirted, essential earth-mother;
only the fire of your hair ash-dimmed, save for the embers
revealed as you unwound, shaking off age.

So I thought of you fondly as I walked by my river –
still with reflection, trees, cloud and sky, until rippled
wind-whispers grew into murmurs, mutterings, chatter of rapids
where sun-glinted wavelets rose salmon-like struggling
vainly upstream, white water-wrapped rocks overwhelmed
by the roar, and back to placid pools of reflection, calm after strife.

And I thought of you fondly with your noisy mill-race where
violence once ripped woollen clothing, fabrics, fleece pieces,
shredding and grinding them down, flocked ready for reworking –
leaving chance gleams of bone, brass, even silver, mother-of-pearl
buttons in the mill-stream pool's mud. Small treasures, but bright
memories to hold after turmoil, in the peace of your garden

where I watched you fondly – surrounded by your flocks:
offspring, friends, cattle, ducks, geese and hens, now
safe in your haven – glad I once knew and remembered
the girl with the sparkle, the smile and the fiery hair.

Hereford Cathedral
(Dupré's Prelude in B flat major)

Seeking shelter from the storm I sit alone
transfixed by music that erupts and swells,
bounces off the ancient walls of stone
seeps through cracks, and slides in waterfalls
of sound that wrap around, engulf the only
person here. The ground beneath me feels
to rise on glorious chords sustained and strong;
the building floats, vibrates with energy.
I doubt my reason as I fly headlong
up to vaulted roof, round chancel, nave; see
half-hid the source of this most wondrous song
an organist almost too young to have achieved
this feat; hold tight as soaring notes subside,
return to earth renewed, to face more rain outside.

Wet Boots and Bottoms

It drizzles in Chepstow, by Tintern
it rains and in Monmouth it pours.
At Symonds Yat stranded, the Wye
in full spate and the ferry adrift. By
Hereford swans stand bewildered
on banks, nests and young
swept away by the flood.

Bedraggled in Hay, I seek
shelter and poems, so sodden
my entry is almost denied.
Only reaching the 'B's' buy
Berryman's 'Henry'
before closing bells ring.

And then at Builth Wells the sun
briefly emerges giving the warmth
I fondly remember in dreams,
but riverside walks are now all awash,
up and down hills becomes a slosh
through red mud, paths are now streams.

I slide and slip my way to Rhayader
and then Llangurig for the final lap
up the valley by an old Roman fort,
through Sweet Lamb Farm's discord
of vehicle noise, past disused mines,
tips and shafts to Plynlimon's heights:
Blaen Afon Gwy, where Wye's waters rise.

Then downhill in sun through forest trails
joining Hafron, the Severn, at present
a stream but soon a full river, and waiting,
my wife with dry shoes and clothes.

Cleopatra on the Oxford Canal

Antony: There's beggary in the love that can be reckon'd.
Antony and Cleopatra Act 1 Scene 1

I walk in a fluster of butterflies, blue-bodied
demoiselles dart black-winged. At my feet
a serpent fat and dark, uncurls, stretches
thin, slides unhurried between foliage, stems,
into undergrowth or water over the edge.

In the shimmer of heat a boat sails towards me,
slowly, out of the sun. On an open front deck
a woman enthroned, bracelets aglitter, neck-
lace entwined, as snakes from Nile's mud-ooze –
Egypt's queen apart from her lover. Transfixed

I gaze as she passes, cossetted, smooth-skinned
from asses' milk, lusted after by besotted men –
imagine she loves me and the beggary of that
reckoned love as silk clad, slim-waisted,
she clasps in soft fingers the slow writhe of asp

that tongue-tips hot-nippled air. Brings it tight
to rise and fall of tremulous breast – I hear its beat.
Would she dare do this for me? Would I when
I heard, fall distraught upon my sword? Or was
it all play, the power of sweet words and the heat?

30°C Near Fenny Compton

Walking the towpath in over-powering heat
I sympathise with fleece-wrapped sheep
forsaking grass for earth, hard-baked beneath
the hawthorn hedge that runs from ridge-top
to water's edge. They huddle close in line,
some stand, some lie, facing uphill, shelter
within a narrow strip of shade while I swelter
in full sun, consoled by aromatic meadowsweet,
and intermittent relief from flickering ash-leaf.

But something jars – a pile of floating debris –
pushing meadowsweet aside I see
an island mid-canal, a dull grey mound
quite large and round, with a smaller lump
nearby and realise this has brown ears
and eyes, wide open, home to crawling flies –
a bloated sheep beyond all help, no doubt
overstretched the metal edge to drink,
with fatal consequence, now ignored by kin.
I hasten to the cool Wharf Inn.

Going Nowhere near Priors Hardwick

In a future post-apocalyptic age
when men and women forage
for their food, they huddle round fires
in stone-tunnelled caves at night;
feast on roots, fruit, leaves, flowers;
gnaw on charred rabbit, rat-meat,
throw bones to hunting-foxes at their feet.

Sometimes they wonder at things:
half-buried ruins of stone, rusting
lengths, strange-shaped metal sheets
beyond their ken or means of working;
contorted, crumpled as by a giant.
Tonight they study a mysterious find:
runes on a white square sign.

Fingers tentatively trace the outline
of red shapes, indistinct and meaningless:
'STOP HS2' 'SAVE COUNTRYSIDE' 'FIGHT'
Later the shaman gives them his best guess:
that "*it came from before 'The Bad Time'.
A curse or prayer to a tribal god known as 'Tren',
worshipped back then when men*

*sought faster travel between here and there,
faster than the vulture in the air
than the wolf running to its lair.*"
When they asked him why, and where
this 'Here' and 'There' was, he had no answer
apart from the legend that "*before 'The Bad
Time' evil spirits drove men mad*".

Banbury Buddhas

Streams spring from the mountains, flow into rivers,
reservoirs, canals, carving ways; trails tramped
by tribesmen, pilgrims, travellers, workers, boatmen,
horse-riders, walkers each exposed to the frailty
of self, connected to earth and water, the totality
shouldering the sky; at home in their loneliness.

Stone Buddhas on boat-homes sit silent, impassive,
serene. No condemnation of the hubbub, of crowds
thronging sacred shopping malls; mild surprise
at the survival of Tooley's old boatyard, embedded,
buried in the retail temple's walls, cramped in the dark
a prisoner restrained or a patient confined behind
curtains, too frail for tears.

Water and walker move on, endlessly seeking resolution.

Waterside Seduction

Late summer and lush growth shows its age
along riverside banks and hedges.
Butterflies, bees sip at ripe berries,
lie idle on leaves overcome with rich juice.

Flowering dog-rose makes a final flourish
through bramble while waterside, pink willowherb,
white fluff of meadowsweet, neat orange-lipped
balsam, compete with blue seeding thistle,
faded dock, its frazzled leaves charred,
and the flaming death throes of cranesbill.

But something stirs in the undergrowth,
creeps, surreptitious as a sly-fingered lover,
reaches forward insistent, takes hold of a limb,
entwines, climbs perversely anti-clockwise,
false feelings declared with a trail of sharp
pointed green hearts, advances remorseless.

Then soothes, misdirects with a tight curled cylinder
which slowly unfurls, opens into an innocent white
full-skirted bell; flirts before moving sinuously on,
always clutching, enfolding in close convolutions,
always reaching for the heights of ecstatic embrace.

And when those are attained seeks further advance,
throws itself forward to the next victim and the next
placing hearts and white bells at regular intervals
until top-heavy it topples, falls among nettles and reeds
carrying all of its conquests down to earth with it.
Rampant seductive ambition leaves hedgerow
and bank festooned with the bindweed's pall.

Pooh-Sticks

Three of them line the rails
of a footbridge over the river –
a girl in her teens, a man in his forties,
an elderly woman. Three generations,
each with a small stick in their hand.

Below them water runs dark
stretching out weeds underneath,
flows towards the roar of a weir.

Sticks are dropped in –
a rush to the other side of the bridge –
the old lady left to fend for herself.
The girl happily claps, the old woman smiles,
her stick is in front.
They follow the sticks.

The man waves his arms, shouts,
jumps up and down
as his stick lodges in reeds.

At the weir a mother and child wait,
signal grandmother, granddaughter
neck and neck winners –
hugs, congratulations all round.

The man follows at a distance,
drags his feet, kicks stones, mutters
to himself – resenting failure, takes
no pleasure in innocent things,
never was young, never grew up.

Travelling Back

At Bath I travel in time, remembering
my youth, tuned in to Radio Luxemburg
late at night under the bedclothes, gaining
access to music frowned on by parents.

The route to Hanham, the end of my trek
where the tidal Avon begins, takes me past
Keynsham, home of the old radio station's
racing tipster. A winning horse guaranteed,
almost, for a ten shilling Postal Order –
'Send today to Horace Batchelor
at Keynsham near Bristol – Keynsham
that's K-E-Y-N-S-H-A-M.'

I go there by train. The name on the station
is enough. Presuming Horace long gone
I press on in rain follow paths over fields,
through a forest of wet Himalayan Balsam,
only horses for company – arrive drenched
to find four houses, two pubs, both closed,
and the lock accessible only from the far bank.
Mission accomplished I walk back to Bath,
the only excitement being threats from a bull
and twice losing my way.

That night at my 'hotel' I go to sleep not
to Radio Luxemburg's sounds but the moans
of a satisfied woman somewhere above.

Passing Time at Temple Meads

The clock painted high on the wall has no
hands, encircled numbers going nowhere.

Transient bodies settle, worry at watches,
consume drinks, food, read yesterday's paper.
Time past passes on. Slow silence ticks
on the non-tocking clock, while outside
grey ghost sea-gulls swoop onto platforms,
peck stray crumbs, small comfort, competing
with pigeons that command the heights
among high iron girders. Waiting, waiting.

Sometime in the future my train will arrive.
It is only a matter of waiting, for time to go by.

If I had looked back I might have seen time moving
silently forwards, to meet me in that long moment.

The Roman Way

O tempora! O mores! Cicero

First steps on a Newcastle road that overlay
the Roman way from Segedunum to Solway
Firth, and a group of girls pass excitedly by –
dressed in bright pink with bunny rabbit
ears and tails – party time for the 'lucky'
one clutching a four foot long inflatable
penis. I wonder what the Romans
might have thought about that.

A week later in Carlyle near journey's
end a group of girls in pink, rigged out
with what appear to be obligatory
ears, tails and penis, pass raucously
by a church where the plaque records
US President Woodrow Wilson's visit.
I wonder again – what his views might
have been. I am slightly concerned
I have been followed the whole way.

Standing Stones

It is there most of the way, once sturdy and strong –
solid stone blocks, quarried, carried and crafted
a barrier running the width of the land – The Wall.

Enfeebled with age, shrunken in height,
its turrets and forts placed every Roman mile
now mainly outlines, reaching knee or waist high.

Plundered over centuries, recycled by farmers
and gentry for farms and outbuildings, field
walls, churches, inns, homes, whole villages.

A wall that was colonised by locals even then
when the Romans patrolled, forts needed extra
hands for smooth running and sustenance.

A wall that stretched over lowland, an obvious
barrier but today what amazes is on the heights
where it clings to the top of sheer cliff faces.

Heroic work to build on the edges of crags, mile
after mile, and why when no enemy could ever
climb up them? Maybe that is the point of it all –
The Wall was always a Statement.

Offerings

Soldiers drawn from all parts of the Empire
loyal to one emperor but allowed to keep
their own gods, some mighty, some cosily
local like Celtic Coventina, worshipped
at her well; some mighty like Mithras
exclusive to officers, both close together
dark and mysterious at Fort Brocolita,

At main fortresses altars dedicated to Mars
or Jupiter needing no more than the inscription
IOM: Iuppiter Optimus Maximusque, the best
and greatest; some like Antenociticus, lesser
known but meriting a statue with altars each side.

And at Fort Aesica, now only faint marks in a field
of grazing horses, stands an anonymous altar
its top covered with coins mossed and mildewed
placed by wayfarers. I add my own offering.

Going on to The Banks, where the Wall once
ended at the wide Firth and Bowness arose
on the site of Fort Maia. There among rubble
in-filling an old farmhouse archway I spot
a possible altar upturned, just another piece of stuff.
Like the Wall itself, little was wasted. Generations
have recycled the hard quarried stone.

Fishing the Firth

Beyond Burgh Church and Drumburgh Castle
fortified with stones from the old Roman wall –
people upstairs, cattle below, protected
from reivers marauding from the north –
men of the south venture towards Scotland
walk at low tide across the Solway Firth.

The lane at Bowness fills with cars, men alight,
walk over fields with rectangular metal contraptions
on their backs – haaf nets, frames net-stretched
too fine to see – trek over sandbanks, water channels
until almost at the far side. Turn to face the incoming tide.

Some individually, some joining in twos and threes
they stand firm in chest high waders as waters rise,
lower their haaf nets in front of them blocking the flow
until from this shore only men's heads are seen.
Patiently waiting the feel of the fish coming upstream
when the net is pulled upwards, salmon trapped.

Catch officially allowed: one each per day, Scottish
Fishery inspectors enforcing the law. Seems profitable
enough to walk half a mile or more out and back again,
to stand stock-still in cold water even if nothing is caught.
It's tradition, the Vikings started it. It must be a man thing.

2

CIRCLING CONTINENTS

Seeking Answers in Antigua

In the market place,
a mother quietens her child,
buys her a glittering multi-coloured windmill;
the child holds the stick;
the wind blows.

Windmill sails whirl,
colours blur, fascinate the child
who sees only a miracle.

Seeking its cause she pulls off the sails,
deconstructs a rainbow,
searches for truth
which blows away on the wind.

The child cries.
The mother of course does not understand.

Anse la Raye - St Lucia

Sweet lush St Lucia green mountain land –
from lowlands, once planted with sugar cane,
banana now spreads; rainforest roads
hurricane damaged, drive up through
the light, air moist hot, green fern
leaves grow wider, trees taller the higher
we go to the Pitons, half-clouded;

Anse la Raye below, neat river-mouth
home of a slave camp in the days
of the French (no cost to the planters –
free water, food from the sea).

Cheap wooden houses, bars huddle
together on straight narrow streets,
locals bustle busy at living, on foot,
on bikes, crowd round the block
outside the butchers for machete
chopped goat – underfoot, cockerels
stalk proud, bright coloured,
scratching hens, chicks –

and everywhere with hang-dog looks
brown dogs loiter, the island breed,
bitches heavily dug-hung –
and trinket-weary tourists hustled
by stallholders. On a shabby seafront
non-descript boats beached like flotsam
curiously named: 'Brothers and Sister',
'Light', 'Ever Friendly' – under nets
hung to dry fowl and dogs snuggle,
bedded into warm sand.

Decay - St Georges Grenada

Nine years since the hurricane, wrecked buildings
still teeter, cling to life. Roofless, without doors or
side windows, stained glass saints still stare out
over the old Anglican altar; eroded memorials on walls
record ancient deaths of worthies, settlers, soldiers.
By tilted iron gates, two lizards watch time pass by.

On a hill, a vast graveyard spreads across
lanes, around outcrops, houses, tumbles down
to the sea. White tombs with handwritten inscriptions
celebrate local occupants: sons, grandmothers;
painted portraits, even likenesses carved,
keep memory warm; the daily ordinariness of death
recorded in dates of life's 'Sunrise' and 'Sunset'.

By the harbour, in an old wooden ruin stripped of worth
and comfort men lounge, drink rum from glass jars,
argue, wave arms; eyed by a mangy dog; wary, forlorn.

Sea King - Grenada

Bright pink flippers float underside up between
low harbour wall and black fishing boat hull;

a splash, they vanish beneath murky waters
dragged down, held by some monster for minutes.

A battered blue cylinder floats to the surface,
strapped to a body tee-shirted black, head

tightly bound in bright spotted bandana
finally followed by pink flapping feet. No

monster but a king of the deep. In his hand
a sceptre, short wooden-shafted, sharp flattened

scraper-blade jammed in one end; now
semi-submerged he works along waterline

inch by inch through sea-growth and rust.
Then down again, lost, out of sight. We return

an hour later; on the quayside regalia heaped,
the royal figure sun-dries, steam rising, enthroned

on an upturned crate. The crown of his labours:
red and gold, blue-black flakes, shimmers on water.

Amazonian Perspective

'Of course, come in, look around.
This our house, our home. See,
we have front door, room with places
to sit, cupboards, kitchen to cook.

Please mind the chickens, dog.
Outside under tree cool place
for hammocks, No, no bed.
No we manage OK. And shower

under water tank, rain very much.
No, no car. No roads, only paths
in the woods, the fields, down
to the river. Canoe boat tied there.

Paddles and outboard motor.
You have big outboard at home?
How can you catch fish then?
Yes, OK, you look in cupboards.

Please, inspect my life, poke
fingers in manioc flour, in spices.
Taste, make funny face. What is
sink? No, we have big metal bowl.

No, we go outside next to shower.
You like it: my life, my home?
I show tourists for a few reals or
dollar please. Thank you. Come again.'

Shoes

They lay alone, abandoned, forlorn,
in the middle of a public square
in Salvador, Brazil: a pair of men's shoes
not new but not badly worn.
Side by side; nothing else was there.

Passing pedestrians walked
around them with care,
as though they had a right to be there,
as one might give wide berth to a statue,
or public monument,
or even a sleeping dog.

The city was preparing for Carnival
but there was no potential gaiety
or fun in the shoes; no raucous hilarity;
nothing to evoke music and dance;
no indication their owner was elsewhere
engaged in establishing mirth or frivolity.
Just two lonely shoes. Abandoned.

In other streets men lay asleep; on benches,
bare pavements, on church steps, curled
up on cardboard, tucked away in corners;
all without shoes on their feet.

city tour rio

between city carriageways
around a grassed strip
men lie
stretched
on low walls under trees
pillowed on stone;
curl from the sun in littered
side alleys
huddled lanes
half-paved;

dogs
scratch
for a meal;
traffic hurtles
clogs
bursts free;
a world bustles hustles a living
scrambles after anything new;

high rise million dollar homes
replace
demolished mean dwellings;
in spaces
between
shanty town spreads
rich need the poor
poor need the rich;

everyone buys
sells;
shopping malls
street barrows;
paint fades
peels
old struggles
to survive;
inside churches
gold saves souls.

I remember Rio

From the mist around Christ's mountain-top statue
a shining beetle flew down. In tears it twitched
its antennae and asked me to help it move on.

This incarnation of a thousand generation old sinner,
having achieved beetle-hood by long good behaviour
had sought the approval of Gautama, the Buddha

to advance further towards full enlightenment
but had mistaken one holy site for another.
When I tried unsuccessfully to console him
he flew eastwards, with deep sighs of resignation.

I see the mountain

I cup in my hands the river of birds:
taste warm yerba maté;
chew assado grilled in markets,
on the ranches,
breathe smoke of eucalyptus.
I revel in the city, its street scenes,
its countryside:
luxury and squalor.

In pocket-park plazas parrots
screech: 'Independence';
bronze men on bronze horses
decorate squares;
opposite Congress, men
without politics sleep on cardboard
under slogan daubed walls;
playboys and girls work
their bodies on beaches,
in tennis and yacht clubs,
on private estates.

Along railway tracks to Peñarol
dogs race the train
full of tourists bemused
by mean homes of breeze-block,
sheeting and planks;
people in doorways, at crossings
stare back at these strangers
blankly aware,
like 'The Last Five Indians'
facing the colonists
in their oxen drawn wagons.

(Continued on page 44)

(Continued from page 43)

As sunset rests on hulks
rusting half-sunk in the harbour
and the mountain behind,
I leave with Uruguay
cupped in my hands.

Battlefield

Across Falkland's wild windswept moors
where men of two nations fought and died,
living and dying continues. Grazing sheep
stray from the flocks, fall ill, die amid peat
or stumble unknowing into minefields:
fleece heaps, stripped bones their only memorial.

Penguin colonies breed, lay eggs, have young
that survive on the fish the parents bring back
once a day, if the caracara bird or weakness
doesn't take them. Flies settle, carcases bloat,
turkey vultures move in; leave only bare skull,
backbone, feet, and small leathery wings
which will never feel the pull of the ocean.

Sheds of rusting corrugated iron
stand near the shore, full of fleeces, rotting
booby-trapped shearings of '82, untouched.
Death still hovers over the islands,
like the vultures, ready to take the unwary.

Glacial Bestiary

In Chilean fjords we marvel at nature's intensity;
vast ice sheets stalk through the mountains,
glacial arms spread, grind down rocks, claw their way,
creep to the sea, tumble piece by piece into the water.
The glacier calves, gives birth.

                        And we imbue it with life.
Our minds see wild-life in frozen chunks of water:
an elephant's head floats by, a unicorn rears its horn,
a dead cow lies on its side legs stiffly outstretched,
monkey faces appear carved in darkened striations,
sunlight bounces back images of toads, an eagle
spread-eagled in snow.

                        Our zoo parade passes by,
turns slowly transparent, glass that vanishes in
its own reflection as water returns to its source.

                        But something moves.
Among the white crystalline debris still floating
four curious dolphins appear: black-backed arches
rise and fall in splashes of foam. Sea-birds dive,
emerge to land on an ice-chunk, flap wings, squawk.
Reality replaces fantasy. We continue to marvel.

Old Dogs of Chile

In every town an Avenida Independençia,
a Plaza de Armas,
a statue or bust of Bernardo O'Higgins;
and dogs. Dogs. Old dogs.
Old dogs litter town squares
on pavements or lawns;
no young ones.

Large dogs, all shades of brown and black,
no particular breed
but never quite mongrels,
lie there, watch the world going by.

But mostly they sleep on their sides
or flat out, nose between paws,
keep company with old men on benches
who try to remember.

One or two dogs will busy themselves:
escort the shadow of a passing soldier
attached either side;
or suddenly stand, shake themselves down
and trot off business-like
on an errand or remembered appointment.

But mostly they lie there
part of the street-scene;
seeming to do little harm,
and no-one bothers to teach new tricks
anymore, to old dogs or old men

Homage to Neruda

I went to Isla Negra
his last and favourite home;
absorbed his presence
from the house, its design,
its furnishings, decoration,
the keepsakes and trivia
so precious to his life.

I sat by his grave and reflected
on the view he once looked out on:
the blue of the ocean;
white-lit foam-surge splitting
grey black rocks on the shore,
his shore; the wind-blown stones
of his imaginings.

I walked on his beach, traced
the brown-cast strands of sea-maiden's hair,
held on to his stones: Las Piedras de Chile,
the skeleton of the land he loved;
found beasts of my own.

I was the traveller who looked for him there,
between stone and ocean, who found him
returned in the churn of the water,
of its salvaged heart.
Discovered and lost
he returned as he promised:
I found him there
in his words,
in stone and in silence.

Dolphins at Isla Negra

Walking the shore
grit between toes
I feel the salt wind's sting,
hear distant cries of resistance
as waves pound the rocks.

Four grey dolphins rear up in a line
backs curved,
noses reach for freedom's air,
tails still embedded in stone.

Long gone the sculptor of words
but his heart still beats
in the break of the ocean;
his voice still carries
in the flurry of sea-spume.

Walking the shore he is near.

remembrance

high in the dry Atacama
where even cacti find it hard
to survive in the burning red stone,
the memories of weary centuries
stand alongside peasant tracks:

tall
thin
stacks
cairns
of
stone
placed
precariously
on stone.

Each an act of presence,
return, remembrance,
preserved by the absence
of wind and rain.
I place my stones on these
ancient towers,
remembering too.

Life and Death in Costa Rica

1

Everywhere life lines: brown paths
trodden into tree bark by generations
of termites right up to the tree-tops;
thin lines of leaf ants stagger down trunks,
clear a track through the forest under green
umbrellas to their underground nest;
black army ants swarm forward,
brook no resistance, take no prisoners,
irresistible on their conquering march.

2

Crocodiles lie still in the wide flowing river,
half-submerged: seventeen nosed in, moored
round a sand-bank, black mud where their captain,
a giant, basks in the sun, legs splayed, yellow mouth
gaping. Close by, a herd of horned cattle, white,
limp-eared, stands on the river bank fanning out
into the shallows. Only above is there movement:
five vultures circling slowly, high over tree-tops,
round and round on the heat, biding their time,
silent, peaceful but ominous, before it cools down;
before thrashing red water, slaughter, gorging.

San Pedro LA

Back Street Eden

In San Pedro LA on a back street down
by the docks, trapped between trash cans
at a beer joint and the wall of a derelict
mart, squeezed in imprisoned by high
chain-link fencing: a 'Garden for Elders'
carefully tended; head-high with green
foliage climb tomatoes in flower,
hang French beans in pod and beyond:
neatly tilled beds, tiny plots of goodness
to come in time, short-lived or long,
berries and lettuce, beet, onions, parsley,
chives, dill and a sunflower struggling
for light upwards to bask in its entitlement,
fit enough to grow, belong, partake here
like an elder, any place, any town, anywhere.

Pelicans

By the fishermen's boats in San Pedro port
pelicans strut their stuff alongside the quay,
cluster and hustle the crewmen as they sort
out their seine nets, wound off, unravelled, laid
on the ground, picking off debris caught up
on the last trip made out into LA bay.
Time and again boatmen hose them away
but experience has taught pelicans
that numbers and persistence pay
until mobs of squabbling gulls overwhelm,
send towards sheds where men fillet, weigh,
ice pack the catch of the day with more
tasty fish bits scraped and washed away
to the pelicans' delight, until gorged
they fly in line over 22nd Street to Cabrillo Bay
The greediest drop near the shore
diving for fish, or bellies filled for the day
fly round the headland to nest sites next door
set against blue an ordered squadron of grey.

Poetry Pilgrimage - San Fransisco

Up along Stockton, past
Washington Square where
Yesterday dog-walkers stood singly
Waiting for pet to piss and sniff,
Today families lounge, play in the sun.

I hit Columbus at Green Street
Minus the Mortuary Marching Band
On to Kearney and the grail, a grain
Of gold in the rush of teeming streets:
City Lights Books, the home
of the Beats, Jack Kerouac, Allen
Ginsberg, Bukowski, Ferlingetti et al:

I enter the haven, clamber upstairs
To the poetry room, two hours
In the sanctuary spoilt for choice;
Come away with Pablo Neruda,
Ferlingetti and Ginsberg,
Pose by the Poet's Chair too modest
To sit in such honoured company.

Muir Woods, Marin County

Sequoia Sempervirens

In Mount Tamalpais' canyon
High stands of redwood, dark
Thick-trunked, bark ridged,
Hollowed out over ages, fire
Blackened, survive the centuries,
Immune to predations of chipmunks,
Beetles, termites; only man can
Threaten, or storm topple
An aging giant, root loosened
Leaving space for a burl to burst
Into new life, hidden seeds sprout
Carry on the ancient family cycle.

Lightbeams

Dappled light shines
Through the high canopy
Down two hundred feet
Past dark-barked redwood,
Over tanoak branches
Fern moss festooned
Through flickering leaves,
Bounces off grey feathers
Of a northern spotted owl
Down through sword fern fronds,
Lady fern, alighting on a single
Flower of redwood sorrel,
Oregon Oxalis
Floating pink on a sea
Of trifoliate green.

Life Cycles

Stanley Park Vancouver BC

Tall cedars, spruce, hemlock have grown
replacing old conifers felled by the loggers.
Deciduous alder, maples grow up underneath.
Signs still remain on great girthed tree-stumps –
notches for springboards, platforms where axe-man
and sawyer worked on past deforestation

but trees shallow-rooted also fall from storms
or just old age and lie grounded waiting,
all havens for mosses, ferns and tree seeds –
nurse-logs to nurture a new generation,

fed by beetle and worm-burrowed wood-rot,
some taken over by racoon and brown squirrel,
roots thrown down envelop the deadwood,
consolidate stumps into themselves,
before forcing skyward.

High on a bare branched hemlock,
two bald eagles perch and mate
with loud clucks, chuckles.
The woods are alive with the rustle
and song of ravens, thrushes,
woodpeckers, finches.

On Beaver Pond silted with lilies,
duck and drake guide
nine new hatched
ducklings, greedily watched
by green slider turtles.

Life comes and goes.

Serenity

Surrounded by deep woods
on paths far from tourists
looking down on the inlet
at Siwash, Vancouver
I see on blue water
a girl on a paddle board
floating, doing yoga –
slowly and carefully
she goes through the motions
body perfectly balanced
while I hold my breath
watching in the silence
until she ends standing
with hands as in prayer –
then picks up her paddle
slowly moving away.
On my high point of dry
land I find a new calm.

The Raven and the Eagle

1

High over Juneau, fly Tlingit clan
Brothers: Raven and Eagle,
Vie over Mount Roberts' hemlock tops,
Circle, swoop, swerve, suddenly drop
Worry each other until Eagle rises,
To check on its nestlings, stays to protect.
Raven dismissively tumbles, somersaults,
Plunges down to the dock front, poses
On railings, glossy black, preening,
Drops to the mussel bed beach, joins
His own kind to forage under pilings.
High above white-headed Eagle still soars.

2

In Sitka, Raven parades on a roof,
Observes the townsfolk passing below,
Hops from one vantage point to another
Warbles and chortles, peers over
To judge the response. Hectors, lectures
If ignored by the citizens; bickers, chatters
With those who talk back. In the bay
High in a tree on a rocky outcrop
Eagle maintains his silent vigil,
Stands watchful sentinel guarding
His brood and the town. Tlingit moieties
In counterpoint give balance to life.

Boston Trio

Old Bones

They're all there in Old Granary Churchyard,
Boston families buried in rows, some
distinguished with upstanding monuments -
John Hancock, Ben Franklin's parents,
but most more modest, even famous sons
of revolution, Samuel Adams, Paul Revere.
Under Hancock's column decked with flags
of the modern republic a small tablet -
for 'Frank, a Servant'. No further name
or back-story, race unknown; the honour
of such personal remembrance forgotten.
Black or white, his bones now moulder
mingled with those of his master, equal -
all bones white, blackened with time.

Derelict Dock

Black rotting teeth, stumped pilings angle
out of water against a rusting quayside,
concrete shattered, weed sown sprouting pink
and yellow. Brickwork faded red, plaster
crumbled, faint lettering bears ghostly witness
to enterprises, lives long-gone. Windows stare
blindly out to sea. A small scene of desolation
and decay, but at sunset, struck by glowing red
and gold, a water-mirrored image exquisite
as any jewel or sacred reliquary.

Safe Passage

Our entry into port and leaving is marked
by bells: a doleful toll rings out its warning,
low insistent measured notes wind and wave
driven, wakes mourning souls long lost
at sea, lying deep beneath waters overlaid
with mist risen from hidden wreck-strewn
depths, where past sailors sound spectral
chimes announcing portals to their world,
invitations we renounce as passing through
the rocking beacons we gain safe passage,
and slow the sonorous ringing fades.

Madison Garden Park NY

Dodging the traffic at Broadway and Fifth
admiring the iconic Flat Iron building
tranquillity is sought in a haven of greenery;
inside that, a shaded sanctum sanctorum
fenced and gated for metropolitan dogs
and their owners, all free and unleashed.

Owners sit and stand in quiet contemplation
or in animated conversation,
men and women in any combination
person-to-person, building relationships,
short-lived or lifelong, all sizes
and shapes all colours and races of people
oblivious to the dogs in their charge.

The dogs, all breeds, all sizes and colours
snooze or cavort, build brief relationships –
sniff, piss, shit, jump on each other, hump
remaining oblivious to their surroundings,
their owners and etiquette as only dogs can;

Elsewhere under dappled shade,
people relax, read books, study maps,
puzzle over distant place names
around the base of the Armistice Memorial,
look up at the flag, the eternal shining star,
photograph against the sun oblivious
to the dogs and their owners.

Audubon's Pond - South Carolina

Alligator snouts cruise through the lily pads
as we admire foliage, birds and tranquillity.

Near the river, sheds where a raft once
transported the whole house a few miles.

A groundsman, freed from his ancestors'
slavedom, keeps the place tidy for visitors.

Civil War stories retold: a plantation untouched
with a false warning notice: "Smallpox – Danger",

like so much of the state, relying on history,
living in the past to keep the flag flying.

3

MISCELLANY

Suffolk Night

Last night I awoke in the dark:
countryside dark, blackness
untainted by yellow pink city-glow,
deep black, spear-pierced shining
bright-silver light, gashes
slashed clear through bleak-black,
holes of white fire so large,
so close I could reach out
and touch them, cup them
one by one in my hand,
gather up in my arms
great constellations, the Plough
balanced on end in the field outside,
giant Orion striding the hen-house hedge
burning fierce, dagger jewel-bright,
backed by vast sparkled curtains of night.

Far too late now of course, but a sight
my mother should have been here
to see, to justify the hours she stood
staring at faint blurred city-lit skies
endlessly asking her question…

Deben Ebb

For David

Between the river's to and fro
life ripples on the tide edge,
mud bubbles with the breath
of molluscs, worms.
Sandpipers surface-prod and feed
while curlews deeper probe
for succulence.
Salt-whitened wrack picked over
by turnstones with no stones to turn.
Across the slow flow
red-stilted oystercatchers
mass-attack mud's fruitfulness.
Life and death move back and forth
in time with rippled edge of tides
between the river's to and fro.

Daisies

For Laura

Bellis perennis perniciously litters the lawn,
closed up in the dark, waiting for heat, for light
to open its ancient day's eye, yellow, white
lashed. Enticed by the sun, children are drawn
to play, lithe bodies flatten white-dotted grass
propped on elbows, legs braced, backs arched.
Faces intent, brows furrowed, eyes
scrunched against sun, darting tips
of tongues peep through nibbled lips
almost too tense to breathe.
Nimble fingers pierce the stem
of each precious hand-picked gem,
threading them one by one to make
a chain long enough to lace
around a wrist or neck, to wreathe
a white and golden diadem
above each happy glistening face
and circle in a joyful whirling dance
celebrating childhood's innocence -
till giddy dreams are shattered. Chains torn,
flowers fall, scatter, trodden, bruised.
Fairy princesses revert to the girls they used
to be, magic daisies common weeds once more.

Dog Dreams

Dreaming, my dog gives noiseless
barks, tongue-tip licks, tail flicks,
legs rhythmically twitch.
I guess he's chasing rabbits or sticks
or cats, but it's only a guess.

Would he ever understand
why in bed I toss and turn
at night, grunt and gurn
as I wriggle, wave my hands?

Would he guess I fight extra-terrestrial beasts,
hack through forests saving damsels, explore,
right wrongs, make love at bacchanalian feasts,
write songs, poems and nightly soar
over mountains on fiery feathered birds,
invent new languages, religions, words?

Of course it is possible that he
actually dreams the same things as me
and can only guess that my dreams consist -
of chasing rabbits or cats or sticks.

Strangers

She was a stranger – we met
on the street. A meeting?
It lasted a second – a fleeting
approach hardly noticed, no words –
a passing of bodies, not touching –
just air between us disturbed
not even brushing –
and maybe a downward glance,
an imagined smile on her face
the lingering hint of a fragrance
as I moved through the space
where moments before she had passed –
face glowing, hair flowing, so poised,
dress swaying, saying…
saying… nothing out loud.

But I needed to know, *now*,
the other woman's reaction,
the one still walking beside me.
Had she read the signs,
seen my flickering eyes
my face muscles tighten
my lips, dry, try to open –
heard my heartbeat quicken?
Would she say *'Do you know her?'*

She must have tasted the smell,
sensed the sensuous walk,
breathed in the smile as well.
I just hoped she would talk –
break the spell,
give me a reason to turn
to look back at the stranger
flicking her hair, swaying her hips
walking assured, bare arms
bare legs, moistened lips.

But she said nothing out loud
as we walked, staring ahead –
leaving a space between us…

Nine Ladies Romping in Stratford-upon-Avon

In the park by the river I could see
in the distance nine ladies standing,
gently moving, turning round in the sun.
As I neared I was taken aback:
for every very mature lady was holding
a tub, dipping in a wire and blowing bubbles;
totally absorbed and rapt in their leisure
as if it was the most natural thing
nine mature ladies should do,

Bubbles: some very small
that died in their infancy,
some more well formed, globes
orange and grapefruit sized
were carried by the breeze,
new worlds shimmering,
while a few ballooned into vast
other worldly shapes, billowing,
aerial jellyfish coated in rainbows.

I could hear their gasps,
oohs and aahs of encouragement,
for the larger or longer lasting,
commiseration for a sudden burst.
I dared not disturb their
intense excitement and walked on.

When I returned their bubbles had gone;
now patiently queuing they took it in turn
to hold onto the strings of a kite
as a friend held it up to the breeze.
A tug and it launched into flight
rising with twists and turns in the sky.
Everyone's face was uplifted, bright;
from the laughter and smiles
their hearts were as well.

What they were celebrating
I never discovered;
being alive in the world
seemed justification enough.

Photographic Memory

I walk into an old photograph today.
You are there – standing, looking sideways,
half-smiling I think, sunlight on your hair.

I recognise the background – Rome
or somewhere with Roman remains.
It could have been Spain or Morocco.

You are not looking at the ruins, just sideways
at nothing in particular, into the distance –
certainly not at me. That would have been posing

and you do not do poses. In the background
the ruins impose, no doubt why I asked you
to stand there – lost in time I needed a connection.

As I walk further into the picture, I see a dog
asleep on mosaics set in the floor – a real dog,
stretched out, brown, short-haired, pointed ears.

I remember now – it was Sicily – just before
or just after I told you. It is not a picture of you
or the ruins – it is of the Sicilian Hunting Dog.

The Knight and his Lady

She lies serene in death, calm,
Resigned, features finely chiselled,
Dressed in plain gown, slippered,
Unjewelled, hair neatly capped
In net, laid on a pillow
Of hard embroidered stone;
Blank eyes stare, no tears
Reveal her fears and hopes long gone,
Cold-bedded now as in those lonely
Knightless nights, years of separation
From her lord who rode away to fight
For Christ abroad in hotter climes,
With sword that cleaved more foreign flesh
Than weapon did his wedded wife
Who stayed behind ever faithful;

And as in life so in death he lies
Apart, at her side untouching,
Grim-faced, helmeted, eyes piercing, lips
Thin under fierce moustache, chain-
Mailed, praying hands clasp hilt
Of sword, weapons, armour elaborately
Decorated, intricately carved,
Redundant sword blade sheathed,
Tip now points down to cold
Soled feet that rest warming on the spine
Of a favourite lurcher, subservient
But touched, loved closer than his wife;

While outside in the churchyard,
Unmarked, forgotten lesser mortals moulder
Close to each other, tumbled bones touch,
Snuggle up together under trodden earth humps,
Jostle in the dark, tug at long grass covers.

Scrimshaw

Deep inside you have left your mark,
incised your presence, scratched images
of yourself, inscribed runic messages
telling of myths, unreliable histories.

Cuts beneath the surface into the bone
leave no outward sign for others to see;
only me. I have felt the scrape of the knife,
the needle's etch inking black lines on white;

whittled, shaped in ways never imagined
as you whiled away time in my mind.

Ring Tones

I rang again today, your voice
saying sorry you're not there,
not available. Whether you are
or not really doesn't matter,
I have no message to leave,
nothing to say that I haven't
said a thousand times before
and no, I do not expect you
to get back to me. But I still
ring just to hear you speak,
hear the sound of your voice.

Maybe one day you'll pick up
the phone when I ring, answer
by mistake thinking it is
someone else, but it won't be.
It will be me and you. Then
what will we say to each other?

Green Man

I live tight behind the blank eye
in a space full of question marks –
hooks of all sizes each with a point
underneath – scabs, bloody blobs,
stabs in the dark, explosive charges,
all asking their unanswered questions.

Marks entwine, tentacles spread,
pulsate, reach out to interrogate,
thorns lock hard-wired, eat into
each cell – out of control, a plague
of uncertainty, all answers giving birth
to more questions, never knowing.

Lines interweave, overflow, seep
through pores, creep over flesh,
cover face, head and neck, sprout
small shoots that burst into leaves –
I cling, trapped in full foliage, dumb,
unseeing, still seeking answers.

The Echo of Ghosts

In the Palace of Alhambra cool waters flow
from fierce lion-headed fountains, glisten
in pools;

breezes seep through fretted woodwork,
pierced stone; play on intricate patterned
tiles;

air scented by almond, loquat, sandalwood
in shadowed rooms where the echo of ghosts
is heard:

men's whispered commands, distant murmurs,
faint-tinkled laughter, women's sighs, women's
sighs.

Where now the Spark

Where now the spark that fuelled the early light
Fired the nerve, the eyes, enflamed the blood
And left us breathless, burning through the night?

My search of crowds to catch the merest sight
Of you, your hair, your face, the smile that could
Ignite the spark that fuelled the early light

And having seen you, sensed the pure delight.
I longed for more, a word and prayed you would
Not leave me breathless, yearning through the night.

When finally we met and held each other tight
The smile, the word, the touch were good,
Here now the spark that fuelled the early light

And lasted, till in thoughtless silence without fight
We drifted helpless on a lovers' flood
That left us restless, turning through the night.

We ought to talk, to touch and smile, that might
Return us to the shore we knew and understood,
Kindle the spark that fuelled the early light
And lead us breathless, burning through the night.

The Other Woman

That Eve! Look at her, how it's turned
out: sons fighting, killing, her weeping,
wailing, giving in to his whims,
him sitting alone talking to himself,
still hearing voices. I would have
stopped all that, it would never
have happened if I'd been around.

Me, Lilith! Shaped from the same ground
as him, grain for grain, not that subservient
moppet made from a bit of his bone.
No trouble with fruit trees and clothes
when we were together, juices mingled
on skin. And all that palaver over my
old pet snake I had to leave behind.

I knew a woman who drowned herself...

in the steamy sweat of the love she sought...
in tears of pain and joy at a new born child...
in the hopes and dreams of her wishing well...
in the suds of washing clothes and crocks...
in the darkening blood of bruised weekends...
in deep swirling waters of debt...
in the vodka and valium of life's frustration ...
in the vast ocean of a world's indifference...
in the weed and flotsam of a city canal...
in spite of everyone knowing

After Joni Mitchell, "Song for Sharon"
'A woman I knew just drowned herself...'

This is not a Pipe

With apologies to René Magritte

Ceci n'est pas une pipe
It cannot hold tobacco
It cannot be lit
It cannot be smoked
It is only an image of a pipe

This is not a pipe
It is a tube of metal
It cannot be stuffed with explosive
It cannot be triggered by a fuse
It is only an image of a pipe-bomb

It is an image of a pipe-bomb
It can teach
It can persuade
It can sustain hatred
It can explode minds

Ceci n'est pas une pipe

Remembering Vincent

1

Still Life – Shoes

(after 'Three pairs of shoes, one turned upside down' 1887)

Dear Theo,

Paris in spring should have been good
for me after Holland – all those peasants
digging potatoes, shifting coal, men, women
and children, stunted, bent, blank-faced,
poorly dressed in their wooden clogs –
rooted in earth and mud, downcast and grim,
although I admit my scene of that family
eating potatoes was one of my best.

I have just finished another, of shoes in need
of repair. They just happened to catch my eye.
The cobbler opposite wants it to hang as a shop
sign – no payment of course but free repairs
for a pair of my own. Have you sold any more
of my pictures, Theo? I am broke and unwell.
I must go south, to the sun, paint cypress trees
and flowers – see if that will brighten life up.

Vincent

2

Through the Window

(after 'Window of Vincent's Studio at the Asylum' 1889)

Outside – blue iris in beds, trimmed grass,
gravel paths, pale lilacs, all neatly ordered,
enclosed by bare plaster courtyard walls.

The artist considers the scene from inside
his room – sunlight reflected through glass
bottles and jars on the window sill, squared
metal bars just beyond the panes – puts down
his pipe on a chair, takes up brushes and chalk
and captures confinement.

casting nets

in oceans of forgetfulness
men cast their nets
seek sleek silver memories
pearls priceless
beyond their mind's reach.

snag on distractions
of bright coloured coral
catch harsh rocks unaware
tangle with mast-heads
long sunken
broken breasts of figureheads.

waves, weeds
hinder
wash over them
as they look down
down
search for themselves
in the holes
from which all nets are made.

On the Evolution of Angels

Do angels come into being fully fledged,
firm-feathered high fliers, free of the fluff
that puffs out the baby bird, capable
of aerobatics from the first moment
of creation; or do they emerge from the egg,
demand food, grow in warm parental
protection, wing-test as they nervously cling
to nest-rim or cliff-edge before taking
that air-shuddering leap of faith, out
flapping down, down, faltering, fighting
life's gravity, to soar majestically heavenwards?

Or did angels evolve from more human stock,
crawl from mud, through knuckle-scraping,
tree-swinging phases, wings develop
from rare scapular eruptions?

Perhaps they began as chubby-tummied putti,
hung from organ pipes, cloud ceilings
turning to flight from necessity. Is the child
the father of the man, for they are all male
or androgynous which suggests some subversion
of the normal process of reproduction?

Are they segregated into their separate orders
at inception or do they move through the ranks
by merit, examinations, earning their wings;
can they be demoted to lower ranks;
is it a job for eternity or only as long
as someone believes in them?

Almost

I am becoming. I climb to the ledge
on the promontory's drop. Flex,
open-armed and wide-eyed,
let the winds take me wherever.

I am becoming. I slide into ocean
absorbing the crystal. Writhe,
ripple wet fur on kelp and dive,
crack open shells, suck deeply.

I am becoming. I scratch at earth
inhaling sweet petrichor. Scrape,
paddle rootwards blind to the future,
tasting nature's raw wriggle.

I am becoming. I hover at sweetness
on honeysuckle's curve. Trace,
tongue-touch the essence of being,
flaunt beauty at lives in the shade.

I am becoming. White-iced,
I glisten on leaves. Uncurl,
shine crisp-fingered cold,
seek new worlds in wet pearls.

I am becoming,
almost transformed,
awaiting the moment,
darkness to light.

A Grammar of Matter

How can the magnitude of life
be explained by pinpoints of light,
particles too small to grasp,
to contemplate?

The infinitesimal so vast,
the vastness a thin veil of nothing,
thick as a gnat's breath.

Hold a magnetic field
in your hand. Pick out the bits.
Watch the rays pass through
you second by second.

Consider the actual existence
of seconds. How thin are they?
How deep a day, how high
a millennium?

How intense are the tensions
in the rigidity of oceans,
the hardness of sky,
the feel of memory,
in the taste of bright sparks
firing the mind?

And then measure love
or describe it.

reflections

the time will come when an old man
stands on the narrow bridge between
now and then, looking down into water
he will stare at the face that looks back
try to identify the stranger –

start as another face
appears alongside
as if looking over his shoulder
a young woman
almost familiar

breeze will ripple the surface
distort the image as it floats away –
settle again as the water shows
only time and an old man's face trying
to remember the drift of the day

The Nature of Things

It is in the nature of things that awaking from mind-
bursting dreams, I wonder with words.

It is in the nature of things that bind-weed climbs
anti-clockwise; that spiders design and weave beauty;
that maple seeds propagate self-propelled on the wind;
that elephants return to the graves of their dead;
that dung-beetles navigate by the stars as they roll
their precious spheres of shit; that snake skin is shed;
that caterpillars dissolve and resolve
into butterfly brilliance; that huddled bees vibrate
muscles to make heat, keep their queen alive in the cold;

It is in the nature of things that as our insignificant dust
speck spins among zillions of stars with the inevitability
of disintegration we still have the ability to care and fight
for a rare plant's survival, a newt's fate, the continued
existence of whales, a common back-garden bird's life,
woodland, an ancient oak tree.

It is in the nature of things we discover otherness in feather,
fur, skin, scales: as waders stab at ebb-mud, circling buzzard
mewls to mate, turnstones turn stones; as eye-glint finds lizard
on heath, snake in grass; as tunnels lead under earth to fox,
badger, moles, worms; as loach lurk in streams; as white blobs
in ponds transubstantiate into the green sheen of a frog's throb;
as bryozoa thrive in sea wrack, encrusted on rocks.

It is in the nature of things to stand on a mountain-top,
imagine other possible lives; see Northern Lights
as dancing souls of the dead; hear songs on wind
wave and trees; feel healing hands in an ocean's warmth;
and alone on wild moors to know there is nowhere to hide,
where we are forced to confront our own selves.